INSCAPES

POEMS
OF INWARD JOURNEYS

SITA KAPADIA

Copyright © 2025 Sita Kapadia

All rights reserved. No part of this publication may be reproduced, distributed, or transmitted in any form or by any means, including photocopying, recording, or other electronic or mechanical methods, without the prior written permission of the publisher, except in the case of brief quotations embodied in critical reviews and certain other noncommercial uses permitted by copyright law. For permission requests, write to the publisher, addressed "Attention: Permissions Coordinator," at the address below.

Paperback ISBN: 978-1-63616-229-4
eBook ISBN: 978-1-63616-229-4

Published By Opportune Independent Publishing Co.
www.opportunepublishing.com

Printed in the United States of America

For permission requests, please email the publisher with the subject line as "Attention: Permissions Coordinator" to
Info@Opportunepublishing.com

Also by Sita Kapadia:

The Woman Beside Gandhi
A Biography of Kasturba, Wife of the Mahatma

Line drawings and cover design by Sita Kapadia

For my beloved family

CONTENTS

Inscapes
Inscapes	12
The Catch	13
Compensation	14
Light the Lamp	15
True Givers	16
Haiku Poems	17

Memories of Long Ago
Seeing Gandhi	20
Mother's Fasting	21
Mari's Mother	22
Then and Now	23
To My Friend	24
To Iris, in Memorium	25
Strategy	26
My Pegasus	27
Kamshet, The Field of Love	28
Rooftop After Twenty Years	30
Grandpa, "Dada"	31
Question Not	32
The Flood, The Ark and The Rainbow	33

Interactive Responses
To Emma Lazarus in Protest	36
Be Sure Now, Krishna	37
Knowing Your Place	38
The Goddess	39
Japanese Tea Ceremony	40
Dollar a Day	42
Footprints in the Snow	43
On Seeing a Sparrow Persistently Pecking at a Mirror	44
Peaches and Cream	45
Prim and Proper	47

The Presumption	48
The Tortoise	49
The Mule Trek	50
To the Bee in Me, and Maybe in You	51
The Cynic and The Philosopher	52
The Pawn	53
The Angle of Repose	54
The Rare Ones	55

Forever Love

Gazelle, My Heart	58
I Am A River	59
I Know	60
Life Lines	61
Not Remembering	62
Radar View	63
Second Thoughts	64
Spirit's Rocket	65
The Body Tune	66
The Skylight	67
Your Face	68
Without You	69

Nature's Way

Nature's Way	72
After the Freeze	73
April	74
The Wonder of Green	75
Spring	76
Wild Flowers	77
Sloughing in Autumn	78
November Trees in The Poconos	79
Mist Rising	80
Claude Monet at Giverny	81
Lessons from Birds	82
Two Birds	83
The Cameo Drama	84

Zebras	85
Zazen	86
The Dew's Farewell	87
Grass Links	88
Trees – My Teachers	89

Contemplations

Awakening	92
Camera Eye	93
Heaven	94
In the Face of the Stars	95
Letting Go	96
The Measuring Rod	97
Speaking of Anchors	98
The Senses and The Self	99
Walking Out	100
Where No Wind Blows	101
The Challenge	102
The Fall Gardener	103
Perspective	104
The Song of The Stone	105
Toward Silence	106
Gourds and Humans	107
The Lotus	108
Meditation	109

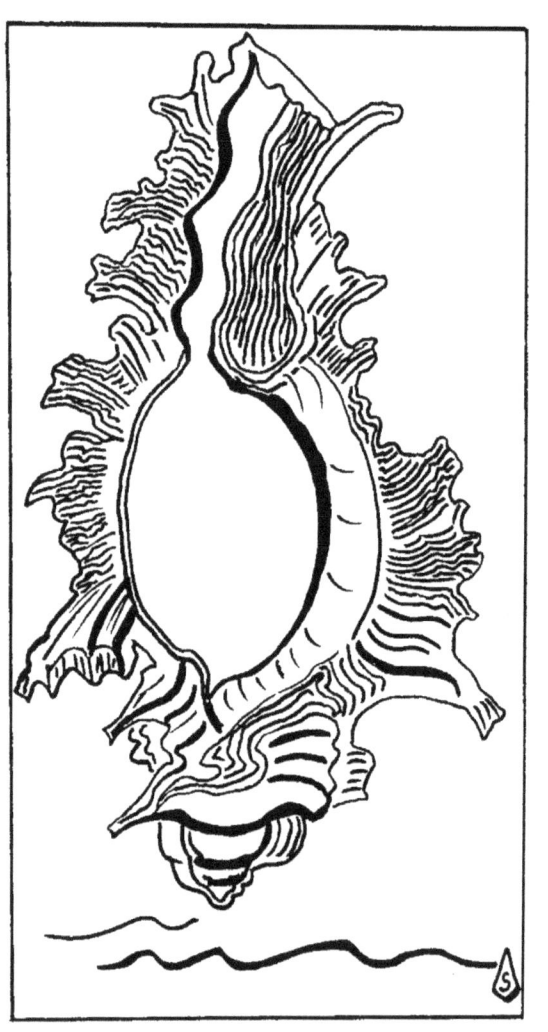

INSCAPES

INSCAPES

Landscapes, seascapes, skyscapes,
All kinds of escapes
Take you off the beaten track,
Ease life's burden off your back,
Carry you off to snowy mountain peaks,
Desert sands and valleys green,
Meandering rivers and seaside retreats,
Thundering waterfalls and woodland creeks
Where light plays with colors of every hue,
Making for fantasy and ecstasy,
And a feeling of dreams come true.

Temporary. All temporary.

But if life's a celebration,
No matter what,
There is no more longing to be gone.
When pathways more mysterious,
More silently spontaneous,
Become a way of life serene,
The mind and heart find expression
Like a joyful fountain where you are.
Then words come rippling in the light.
A happy happenstance it is for me,
And because they come from an inner realm,
"Inscapes" is my name for them.

THE CATCH

When fish
Hibernate in frozen lake
Darkly opaque and still

I wait
Patient daily for early thaw,
A cracking in the ice.

I watch
For ripples under the surface,
A sudden trembling light.

I throw
A line and sit attending,
My heart strung out on a spool.

I pull
On the bite strong and steady,
Heady for what might out.

I catch
The slippery, living thing –
A poem.

COMPENSATION

Helen Keller had no eyesight.
She had compensation, though.
She said, "What is worse than
no sight, is no vision."
And she had vision as well as insight.
Beethoven was deprived of hearing.
But he felt melodious vibrations
That he rendered into symphonies
To the delight of generations.
So, if we, one and all, would but explore
Where we lack, and where we're enriched more,
We'd explore, explore,
And weep over less, no more.

LIGHT THE LAMP

In this our sad and insecure world
Torn apart by vengeful warfare,
Poisoned by mistrust and hate,
Let me not despairingly lose faith.
Let me, in my heart, light the lamp.
Light the lamp, oh light the lamp.
Put in it the wick of courage,
Pour in it the oil of love,
Light it for the flame of faith.
Oh light the lamp in the heart,
Light the lamp.

TRUE GIVERS

The river is a giver
So too the sunshine
So too the trees.
Giving freely to one and all
Is their essential nature.

Can it be that I alone
Go out and get things
For me and mine
Accumulate, accumulate
And stand apart from nature?

Sure, it's good to give
In cash and kind.
Yet, is it enough, I wonder.
True giving must be of one's self
Like the trees, the sunshine and the river.

Supernal spirit residing within,
Kindle in me true giving
That I may with love abundant
Fulfill my own essential nature
Like the trees, the sunshine and the river.

HAIKU POEMS

White fog horizon
ship's horn sounds a distant call
a flapping of wings

---

deep snow in frost light
makes moons of rhododendrons
music of spheres

---

in white shrouding mist
bent old tree clings to old rock
life's calligraphy

---

seeds sunk deep in earth
are stirred by rain ravishings
green fields tell their love

after grey winter
burst of forsythia bells
soon spring will appear

---

frozen water thaws
red gold shining sun above
red gold koi below

---

white herons in spring
alight on cherry trees in bloom
Ah! enchanted eyes

---

when trailing willow
weeps over bridge and water
brush in hand I gaze

MEMORIES OF LONG AGO

SEEING GANDHI

That day in 1946 remains luminous
though decades have gone by,
some slow, some fast,
with life variously unfolding,
through war and peace,
subordination and freedom.
But one experience remains
a constant glow –
The day I, a child of nine, saw close by
Gandhi's face with that unforgettable glow,
at a prayer meeting, rosary in hand.
"Mahatma – Great Soul" they called him,
and rightly so.
That memory brings a drum beat
strong and persistent in the heart.
"Do some good!" The drum beat says.
"Know the Truth."
"Teach the Truth as best as you know."
Remember that glow that welcomed all
To love the world as one peaceable family.
Let us remember to bring that glow
In our lives with Truth and Love,
always with Non-violence and Peace,
Compassion and Service.
Never, ever forget that glow.

MOTHER'S FASTING

Mother fasts three days a week, or more –
Mondays for mindful meditation,
Thursdays for increasing knowledge,
Fridays for unconditional love.
Also, the eleventh day of the waxing moon,
And the eleventh day of the waning moon.
The five organs of perception,
The five organs of action,
And the one mind makes eleven.
Controlling all makes potent the fast.

Also, all holy days that fall on other days –
Tuesdays to counter all raging martial aspects,
Wednesdays to foil untoward mercurial change,
Saturdays to ward off sitting saturnine gloom,
Sundays to invoke benign energies of the sun.
On those days she knows no hunger. None!
In the posture of prayer humble I see her,
Hoping for fullness, prepared for emptiness.

Ancient chants ripple as waves on the sand.
The silence within, who may understand?
I wonder at no need and no hunger,
No private plea, nor protest in prayer.
I see in the unsounded depth of her fast
How the ocean heart lulls personal hunger,
As hungerless she goes singing through her fast,
So that all she loves may have a full repast.

MARI'S MOTHER

Mari said, her eyes distant yet intent,
"A formidable specter is Mother now,
A body so frail and incontinent,
A swaddled wisp in an ample bed.
She holds on fast to life, somehow,

Mother, in charge, gave no commands.
Now, helpless, she makes me take pause
Involuntarily in my anxious race
Against time to make a difference,
To help shape the world sans violence.

Now, fading, she wields more influence,
A wordlessly loud pronouncement
That stirs me to turn inward my radar
To see myself in her, my child in myself
On bended knees at life's inscrutable altar

THEN AND NOW

He loved to hoard glass marbles
And I all pretty beads.
And few things were so precious
That we would not trade for these.

Then suddenly ascetic,
He gave up marble brawls,
And I bestowed my treasures
On pigtailed little gals.

For he and I, we told ourselves,
Had quite outgrown things petty.
Eternity held her sides, laughing
At the joys of our maturity.

TO MY FRIEND

Our meeting is picnic on the grass
where minds lean one against the other
and our thoughts, like children,
run their separate ways
and return flying birds
trilling new discoveries,
urging,
come along with me, come and see!
And so we advance in mind,
as we do in time.

TO IRIS, IN MEMORIUM

I see you, Iris, in the springtime,
In summer, fall, and winter too,
Not only when spring iris bloom, but
When the spirit's verses seek a rhyme.
Your voice low, soft, judgment-free
And I, unthreatened, saying my rehearsed line.

In big round blues nothing new to see,
But yours were laser, listening eyes.
They invited me in, that I might meet
Myself – the self slipped away from me –
The self seen in a flash by a stranger,
You, whom I knew not then, nor how you saw
My tethered pinions bruised in captivity.

You took the briefcase from my uneasy hand
And put in place of it a book of verse
And all the sweet air, the unmeasured sky,
The sweet yielding earth, and oceans still unsounded.
You put them all back in place for me, dear friend.
When some casual passersby ask if I knew you,
How might I say yes and more, and hope they'd understand?

STRATEGY

As a child on Chowpatty beach
I made sandcastles,
Turrets with trumpeters
And tunnels down which marbles rushed
Like royal chargers bearing down to victory,
And when the tide came rushing in,
Threatening to raise to level ground
My palace proud, I deftly built
A deep, wide moat around my castle walls,
Safe till sundown of that day.
In those days I used to know what channels
To design, what spades to put to use,
So that my love's castle, my work's world
Might stand unswept by the tide.

MY PEGASUS

That Indian summer,
he waited every brisk morning,
stomping to be on the road,
bent on doing his own thing,
as it were,
and I in a small way partaking.

For it was his will
along the red earth trails
of woodland Matheran,
in the Western Ghats of India,
to points Monkey, Hart and Louisa,
One-Tree-Hill and Panorama.

Racing himself
up from King Arthur's Seat,
the breeze in his mane and tail,
the air electric with his intent,
the ground under, resounding,
his iron legs pounding.

White star forehead,
chestnut body in movement,
at ease still sinewy,
as when he bent his stately head
to eat lump sugar
from my friendship-seeking hand.

It seems I was not his feeder,
nor, in a sense, his rider,
as he was mine.
I the hopeful flyer,
he the strong-winged Pegasus
vaulting the sky with self-possess.

KAMSHET, THE FIELD OF LOVE

The Field of Love is what it meant, did Kamshet,
where once my family spent a summer.
I sat on the knoll by the slow-moving river
in the dappled shade of a mulberry tree,
and wrote love all day, read love all day,
idyllic day, idyllic night for a lover and a dreamer.

One night, though, a piercing scream
invaded the silent night, unruffling sweetness
with one long, chilling inroad into the inviolate
sanctuary of sleep – our sleep. I deemed
some poor wretch huddled on a cow-dung floor,
suddenly aroused by a stinging scorpion bite,
shrieked out with pain to no one in particular.

It happens all the time; nothing we could do.
Once again then darkness reclaimed the placid air.
And once again we slept as we did before,
there in the languid lotus land by the sleepy river.
It must have been a perfect Indian summer,
there in the charmed field of love, Kamshet.

Sequel, thirty years later.

"Let's go there, Mom," you said at the wheel.
"It isn't far and I've always wanted to see Kamshet."
"It may not be the same, you know," I said,
for some unfathomed reason resisting a visit
to a place from my youth, when life was as yet
a dream in the making, or the make-believing.

"I can just see you, Mom, under that big mulberry,
looking down at the river, gazing up at the hills,
and writing to Dad. Now your son is standing
at this very spot. Pretty incredible, isn't it?"

"Yes," I said. "It's incredible too that most of all
I remember a villager's scream from a scorpion sting.
Nothing we can do about it, we had told each other.
I think of it often now, and I wonder, and wonder."

ROOFTOP AFTER TWENTY YEARS

Remember how at the rooftop restaurant
We danced touching heaven on light feet.
The band played "So near but so far away"
All violins, trumpets, cymbals, drums
Struck up at once and have not stopped.
Stars came out close surrounding your head
Entering my eyes
Making the world strange
Star-spangled, iridescent
With laser beams
That bore through my heart.
And you, though now familiarly near,
Still have the music making touch and smile,
And I with a constant melody in my heart.

GRANDPA, "DADA"

You are like Elmer's or is it Crazy glue?
You mend all big or little things,
Anything too painful to remember,
Anything that seems a "never again venture".
All, all come together with no cracks showing.
You do not have to work at it painstakingly.
With you it is simply natural.
In mending, you make new too
By your touchstone chemistry
That breathes polluted air and gives it back
Processed, purified imperceptibly.
And you, free of pride, know not what you do.

It is as cool as singing a silly little jingle,
Or getting ice cream on the way home from school.
Because you, Dada, are always there
Like gravity - dependable, level and more.

QUESTION NOT

While she went on pilgrimage
And knelt to Him in prayer,
The Lord took in the prime of life
Her buoyant husband dear.

I remember that bereaved face,
Not smiling, not crying,
Those sleepless, staring, eyes
Oft questioning God's grace.

Puzzle not over His ways, dear sister,
For He works in mysterious ways.
And when to His will you surrender,
A miracle may well appear.

THE FLOOD, THE ARK AND THE RAINBOW

Ages ago when incessant rain
Poured by day and by night
Flooding a vast expanse of land,
A heavenly ark provided sanctuary
For a chosen few.
When at last the rain ceased
And the sun heralded a bright new day,
A magnificent rainbow appeared on high
Signifying promise of happier days.

In our own time, when came the rain,
And more and more stormed in upon the land
Till the land was flooded,
Roads became rivers, reservoirs could contain
Their water no more, and rivers
Leapt far beyond and above their banks,
People's homes were flooded, forcing them to flee.
But our house, by divine grace, was a safe haven,
An ark with water all around.

After seven days the sun appeared in all its glory
In a cloudless blue summer sky.
"Now where is the rainbow for us?" I asked.
A voice, a still small voice made answer,
"Look not for a rainbow in the sky,
But in your own self. The seven colors
Are qualities of your own head and heart.
Truth, love, non-violence, compassion,
Faith, hope and service. A potential rainbow
For one and all.

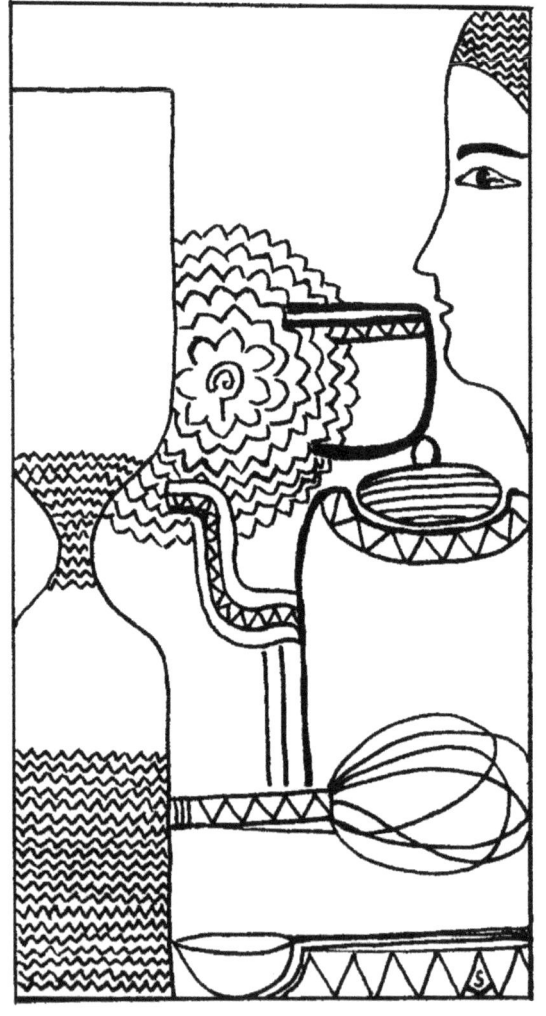

INTERACTIVE RESPONSES

TO EMMA LAZARUS IN PROTEST

I too along with you in unison
Sing the praises of Lady Liberty,
Her welcoming bosom and extended arm,
Her freedom flame bequeathing dignity.

But in the midst of glorious rhapsody,
One discordant note from you – "wretched refuse"
Of another shore – that, not prosody,
But worse, jars on my more uplifting muse.

Treasures of India I brought to share
To add to the riches of America –
Two lands to me as mother and father
And I their robust East-West daughter

With the truest marks of the immigrant –
A spring in my step, a song in my heart.

BE SURE NOW, KRISHNA

Be sure now, Krishna
To live up to your Thousand Names.
All-awareness, All-pervasive
In all who wake and sleep and dream.
Consciousness sans beginning, sans end.
Father, Mother, Child, Demon-slayer,
Teacher and Lover, Miracle worker,
Flute-player, Adorer and Friend.

By Jamuna banks I heard
Your flute's inviting melody
In Gokul and Brindaban
I saw You Peacock-feathered at play,
Your face the sky's own April blue,
Your adornments, your yellow garment,
Golden as the all-bearing Earth.
Sky, Earth, Water - all were You.

Be sure now, Krishna,
Omnipresence, to be here too
By this vast, cold Atlantic shore
With conch-shell, wheel and mighty mace
On Hudson banks and Staten Island.
Shine, Bright – countenance, through wintery haze,
All around skyscraper grays.
Show me your steps upon this land.

Be sure now, Joyful,
To live up to your Thousand Names,
Lord of creatures, Bliss, and Love,
In-dweller, Vast, Space-spanner,
Strength of the strong, Wisdom
Of the wise, Friend of the poor,
Compassionate God, impersonal Om,
Be here now, Formless-form.

KNOWING YOUR PLACE

If you would but only know your place,
Curb your ambition for others' domain,
You would not have to suffer so much pain –
Stepped on, passed over, treated as menace,
Or garbage. You would never have to know
The raw wounds of wrenching separations,
Aborted babes, or ruthless evictions.
Annoyance grows as bigger you grow.
Your forward strides are called transgressions.
Resentments rise, though with you no fault lies.
I, for one, hold you in high estimation
As any impressive, showy focus of all eyes.

Some say, "She speaks of women of these days -
So forward, over-reaching, crossing bounds!"
Well, I know I am just speaking to you, Mentha,
Spade in hand, in my beloved garden.
Wholesome, perennial, primal perchance –
Spearmint, peppermint, applemint and more -
Everyone, in spite of all, a bright survivor
Raising proud, pretty head with nonchalance.
But in my words, admiring your forward darts,
Undaunted in every well-guarded place,
Some may hear thumpings of their own guilty hearts,
That hardened long, hurt now for lack of grace.

THE GODDESS

Art critics and art historians crowd the exhibit hall
Craning their necks around photographers
For a closer look at Parvati, the goddess carved in stone.
Students muster around art professors,
Pronouncing in their knowledge-professing drone,
"Here from ancient India comes to our shores
this epitome of erotic art. As you may notice,
the female figure is represented in voluptuous
proportions.
Nothing like it exists in far Eastern or Islamic art.
Nor, for that matter, in Christian art. In Indian art there is,
as in all traditional arts of India,
no separation between religious and secular art.

To me, standing apart, yet listening,
she is neither overtly erotic, nor covertly suggestive.
She is the goddess Parvati, daughter of the mountain,
Spouse of Shiva, the eternally pure, in the world but not of it,
whose son is the elephant-headed Ganesha, remover of obstacles,
supreme, non-violent power.
She is no stone. She is meaning beyond meaning.
Her full bosom is mother Parvati's promise
to nurture you and me, and all everywhere,
for all life, the whole earth is but her substance,
our limbs are her primal energy, resting or acting,
our mind and heart, her strength.

Erotic, did you say, professor?
Ah, your eyes see the body lines, mine see beyond.
I know her pulse is my pulse,
though she stands here in stone.

JAPANESE TEA CEREMONY

Come to the Teahouse, come, drink tea.
Come, partake of a feeling deep and simple,
Too deeply simple to surface in daily busy-ness.
Take off your street shoes, shake off dust from the road.
Bend low to enter the timeless world of Now.

Enter a bare room, at once artful and precise,
With straw mats and an alcove of nature,
A calligraphy scroll and a flower.
A place to sit at on bended knees,
A place for reflective pathways in silence.

What says the white chrysanthemum?
"Though tomorrow I will die,
And yesterday I was unseen in my bud,
Today I am here! Nature is new every moment,
Now is the moment!" it says.

The tea hostess enters, sliding doors.
Measured steps scrape the surface of the mat.
Listen! Listen for silence in sound.
She offers you a sweet wafer, not sumptuous,
but enough.
Eat it as though only this matters Now.

Again and again she wipes tea things –
Kettle, ladle, bowl and whisk of yesterday's grime
With a napkin folded arrow-like for focus.
She pours hot tea unhurriedly like a slow stream
Intent upon emptying into fullness.

She holds the ladle up to her face,
A mirror for sight turned inward,
From inwardness out again to fullness.

She offers you tea – thick, bitter, green tea frothing hot
To savor slowly, bewailing not the bitter potion of life.

She shows the way of tea – drinking from a bitter or empty cup.
Smiling, with her pointed napkin she folds past and future into Now.
She says, "Ichigo Ichie", This is your first time,
This is your last time – one moment, one meeting
In a cup of eternity.

DOLLAR A DAY

Dollar a day comes to 365 a year
366 in a leap. Not a big sum to clothe
one deep-eyed skeletal child, provide clean water,
food, basic education, immunization.
No, not at all. If I could I would, for sure.
If I win the lotto – gosh! What I've spent on that
twice-a-week hope of big takes – I could pay it all
at once, not for just one kid, but more, many more.
Let's see. Notepad in hand I jot down expenses.
Mortgage, utilities, insurance, cars, gas, grocery.
How they add up, just basic priority things.
Clothes, dollar movies, occasional dinners out
To relieve stress and drab of daily confines.
And birthday, Christmas, Diwali gift-givings.
Also, Mother's Day, Father's Day, and Valentine's.
Besides, doctor and dentist bills, co-pay medicines.
And then, emergencies. It gets pretty scary.
No! No! I had better not commit myself long term
to Dollar a Day, thirty bucks a month for that.
I turn face-down the scrawled-over hopeless notepad.
Won't work. I had better get some chores done instead.
I yank out the vacuum cleaner, the old rattler.
I push and pull, push and pull. It swallows
only surface dust, makes but the surface clean.
Busy noise. It won't outsound the din in my head.

FOOTPRINTS IN THE SNOW

After that crisp evening
With the rare purplish pink light
In a translucent, cloudless sky,
In the silence of the night,
It snowed.
I darted to the window
Crying joy at the expanse
Of freshly fallen snow
On rooftops and trees and on the ground.
Enlivened by a blanket of shimmering white,
My wilting, grey garden was suddenly transformed.
The gazebo in my garden was a sheer delight,
As though it were a magical, crystal shrine.
All around, wherever the eye caressed the landscape,
There was snow,
As perfect as I want my actions to be,
As flawless as I want the future to be.

And then I saw them –
A cat's footprints in the snow.
A bird's are too faint, a dog's too hurried and flayed,
But a cat's footprints in the snow
Are something else,
Something fixed indelibly in memory,
Firmly rounded, measured, deliberate,
Proudly saying to all who pause to look,
"I was here!"

Would that I too, in my passage through life,
Leave footprints that make a difference,
A real difference, however small,
That I, looking back, might happily declare,
"I was here!"

ON SEEING A SPARROW PERSISTENTLY PECKING AT A MIRROR

You chirp and chirp and chirp again,
You almost seem to weep,
There's no response, and yet you cry,
Chireep, chireep, chireep.

Your own shape mirrored so, brave heart,
It's strange that you should court,
And spend imploring hours to peck
At what is. Yet is naught.

We too, like you, little sparrow,
Go after a mirage that lures.
Perhaps it is wiser far to seek
That which serenity ensures.

PEACHES AND CREAM

One rare metaphysical morning,
when my mind had forgotten my body
and like some night-blooming water lily
folding in upon itself at break of day,
turned toward inward centering,
my neighbor, the cosmetics lady, came.
She slipped in the door insisting
on flourishing a magic wand
over my unpainted head.
She claimed she had everything
I could possibly want.
Everything? I asked, intrigued,
thinking of things that do not come
in boxes or bottles or cute little jars.
Do you like a sheer, translucent
or matte finish? she asked,
nimbly spreading out her wares –
boxes and bottles and cute little jars.
It sounded like transcendent.
Oh yes! I'd like to go beyond
The mundane, if I can, I said.

Tell you what, she rejoined with a beam,
I've just the thing for you –
I'll put you down for Peaches and Cream.
So I was instantly transported,
as in a vision or a dream,
to the valley of perennial peaches
and to the sacred Kamadhenu cow,
that yielded creamy milk.
But once again her voice, like silk,
caressed the air in gushes,
We have everything for a new you –
extra length eyelashes,
and highlight shadow collection

for a new, out of this world, exciting you!
Out of this world? I asked, intrigued,
Not new, though, simply with things you put on?
I doubted. She zealously reassured,
That's just the point. It's true.
The order will be in, in two weeks' time.
Bet you can't wait! she said, engagingly
flashing her salesgirl's smile.

I flashed back at the mystic prodigy
with intimations of facial immortality.

PRIM AND PROPER

Our good miss Prim and Proper
Knew all answers, great and small,
What to do and speak and think

And the manner of it all.

Emotions whatsoever
Were such a nuisance to her.
Where she dwelt, stern Reason dwelt.
None other dare approach her.

That is why, one fine Sunday
We heard the strangest story –
(But beneath the tranquil top
Great unsounded depths may be) –

That our good miss Prim and Proper
Turned revolutionary:
She ran off with some old man
She bothered not to marry!

THE PRESUMPTION

Did he think
She'd grow grey
Because he said nay?

There's morning still
And evening
And work in the day.

There's baby talk
And a country walk
And the pure joy of play.

There's friendship and family,
Soul-searching worship,
And helping the needy every day.

To be sure,
She will grow grey.
But not because he said nay!

THE TORTOISE

Come gentle petals
Come stones ungracious
Steadfast you sit
Staid tortoise.

Awake, aware
And well-withdrawn
Into the quiet dome
Of contemplation.

In awe I watch
Your unperturbed
Self-confident
And measured tread.

And hope to build
Deep within me
A peaceful sanctuary
Inspiring actions just and free.

THE MULE TREK

Untrodden snow lies above
Himalayan passes where
Mule carries load upon load
Of assorted stuff
On a dizzy mountain trail
To the motley bazaar.
His head is bent to the ground.
His eyes lack luster.
When he stops at last
In this routine rut,
He eats chick peas from a sack
Hung like gallows noose
About his straining neck.
Mule has never lifted up his eyes
Above his beaten trek.
To see snow-blazoned peaks,
That spark an inner flame.
Mule trudges and eats.
Mule eats and trudges.
They laugh at him that know not
That they too do the same.

TO THE BEE IN ME, AND MAYBE IN YOU

Busy bumble bee,
Know you not humility,
Broadcasting so incessantly
Your routine industry?

Look over at the butterfly nearby,
Flitting about, so gently pollinating,
From flower to flower silently,
Unaware of its delightful beauty.

Evanescent as a sunset,
Seen one moment, gone the next.
Yet lasting always in the mind,
Bringing joy it leaves behind.

Come! Come! Busy bumble bee,
Stop that zig-zag buzz and bluster.
Just do your bit in silence,
And look around in wonder.

THE CYNIC AND THE PHILOSOPHER

The cynic and the philosopher
Once shook hands over a wager.
Which of the two, they argued,
Was the better lexicographer.

Love, said the sour-faced cynic,
Is a code word used by cheaters.
And though all lovers are cheaters,
Some cheaters are philosophers.

The philosopher, he parried,
That cynics may scoff and sneer,
But love is a universal panacea
Except for cynics, the stubborn nay-sayers.

THE PAWN

In this game of chess
I am but a pawn,
the smallest.

Yet, zealously I may
Travel quite far
or farthest.

And needless to say
That in the embattled fray
I must not lose my head.

Or barely getting there
I must never despair
but proceed undaunted.

And never once imagine
Myself to be the only
anointed clod.

But always on the faithful plod
Let me get across this board,
my guide, The Lord.

THE ANGLE OF REPOSE

The engineer assured me my house, a cliff-hanger,
Was safe, positively stable.
"When you turn over a bucket of sand,
The sand settles at a certain angle.
That angle is called the 'angle of repose'.
A house like yours built on the angle of repose
Is secure, tremor free, you know.
You have nothing to worry about whatsoever."

So he said with a wide flourish and a broad grin.
But I was not as concerned for my house of brick and mortar,
As the house of my being, where mind storms begin
And shake and threaten the foundation of selfhood.
For the sharp gradient, truckloads of landfill are needed.
But what truck holds
Love, patience, courage, contemplation,
Preparedness without skepticism – faith,
Work without attachment to reward - yoga of action?

These I try to unload, spade by spade,
Till the steep slope becomes gentle and I am
But when –
What second, minute, hour, day,
What week, month, year, decade,
What century, what birth
At last on the angle of repose?

THE RARE ONES

Some there are that bite
Those who fed them in their plight.
Then there are the smug majority
Who live in measured reciprocity
And a few rare ones
There are who stroke and comfort
Even those that dealt
The blows that hurt.
Rare! So rare!

FOREVER LOVE

GAZELLE, MY HEART

Gazelles
beautiful beings
long-legged
keen-sensed
swift and restless
roam the savannas
all day
every day.
Now they pause and listen
now they scan the sky
and now again they startle
and take off
leaping across
the same green reaches
toward the horizon.
Gazelle, my heart
lithe-limbed
all eyes
all ears
and thoughts of you savannas vast
that stretch beyond
day journeys to the end of time
to spaces not bound
by meridians of the mind.

I AM A RIVER

I am a river of love.
You are my ocean of joy.
Long ago,
since the flood gates of the heart
burst open,
my waters have flown one way –
your way.
Nothing will turn them back,
no matter what,
for rivers dream of oceans
no matter how long the way,
rugged, steep or slow
to the mingling of waters.
Separate bodies,
in dream inseparable,
sweet repose of soul,
long journey's end in ecstasy,
for oceans welcome rivers;
they receive them into their wide embrace,
and rivers, mingling forever,
no longer roam,
for they know they are home.

I KNOW

Somehow,
When you're in town,
I know,
For the leaves on trees
All greener show.

Somehow,
When you're in town,
The road
Is but a step to go,
The load, no load.

Somehow,
When you're in town,
The very air
That stood listlessly about,
Turns debonair.

So, you see, I know.

LIFE LINES

They read tea leaves
in the bottom of tea cups
I too look for patterns of promise
life's cup drunk to the dregs
in cryptic configuration
your face my fortune

NOT REMEMBERING

Do I remember you?
No, I do not remember you.
I do not bear in mind
my breathing in or breathing out
my blood coursing down my veins.
I cannot remember you,
for I remember only that
which even for a moment I have forgotten.
I do not remember myself,
I do not remember you.
After deep sleep,
before I know where I am,
what day it is,
or even who I am,
I see you.
Therefore, I say
I do not remember you.

RADAR VIEW

If I were to look
Into the radar of my heart,
What do you think
I would find in view?
Farthest, near and nearer still,
You, you and you!

Swifter than the swiftest,
Closer than the closest,
Here, there, everywhere –
You, you and you!

But this is, so to say,
Only wishfully true,
For you are gone up there
And I am with my memory radar down here.
Alone. And yet, miraculously
In memory, never alone.

SECOND THOUGHTS

Yes, I would want to be suspended
in vast emptiness in a space suit,
be one in ten or twenty million
chosen for purposes of scientific pursuit.

Yes, I would want to contemplate
earth and existence from out there,
ponder on life, death, essence,
with a previously unimagined flair.

Yes, I would want the experience
of distance or of detachment,
or of my diminutive self in space
through a rarified experiment.

But, if these require leaving the pull
of gravity and gravity is you,
well then, let such profundities wait,
while I dally right here with you.

SPIRIT'S ROCKET

As it curtsies to the wind
Or stands in yellow brightness,
This slim laburnum in sun-bloom,
Somehow, like you, dispels all gloom.

Whether I caper down the lane
My heart at happy canter,
As heady with long draughts of joy
As any waltzing butterfly,

Or in dejection drag slow feet
As though the sun were in grey retreat,
If there's but semblance of your face
My spirits rocket into space.

THE BODY TUNE

Dance teacher says she'd love to have me in her class,
truly a great honor. Oh no, think I, she wouldn't
find me as nimble of body as of mind. I couldn't
stretch, bend or flex like that. Her walk is dance,
her talk is dance, her gestures, eyes, hands are dance,
even her neck stretch on tiptoe is dance, while I
strain to coordinate, creek, stiffen and suffer pain.

Both of us have seen the same long seasons pass,
when for me words awoke with meaning and nuance,
for her came meaning in movement through her dance.
She says I too this late could glide and glance with
pluck.
I too could sing the body electric. My own.
So I go to dance class and feel in tune one day and not
the next, a swan one day and then a waddling duck.

I stretch limbs that rebel against my longing
to say with my body what my heart feels deeply.
I celebrate supple grace, bewail sudden slack.
In dance I have not yet facility to make my own melody.
Yet I have heard as though only I and I alone
Through all the world have heard such a body sing.
Yes, in your close embrace I've heard it. My own.

THE SKYLIGHT

Here in my rocker I sit, Beloved,
And look up at the skylight
Where you used to love watching
The tops of trees, picture-framed,
Bend or sway or stand motionless
In a rectangle of changeable sky –
White, blue, pink, gray, white-quilted,
Sometimes a silver moon cradling.
Trees up there are rootless, trunk-less,
As though to terra firma unrelated.
Only that part of their being
Lives, that forever touches the sky,
As though forever touching,
Like me, the face of their beloved, Beloved.

YOUR FACE

The lidless eyes of memory
Fix me with their gaze.
I miss a heartbeat
And every time the gap
Is filled up with your face.

WITHOUT YOU

Without you, nothing
That's what I thought
When you were no more
In the flesh, living.
Like a hill in dense fog I was.
No sun, no moon, no stars,
No thought of living.

Then your parting words
came to me loud and clear.
"I want you to live just the way
you have been living with me.
Be yourself. Happy, creative,
Loving people. Be with people.
Rejoin your Garden Club. Do your writing.

You spoke more than your breath
could let you. By the time you stopped,
I knew the truth of your words.
There's much to do.
Life with you is worth remembering,
cherishing. But life without you,
is not nothing.

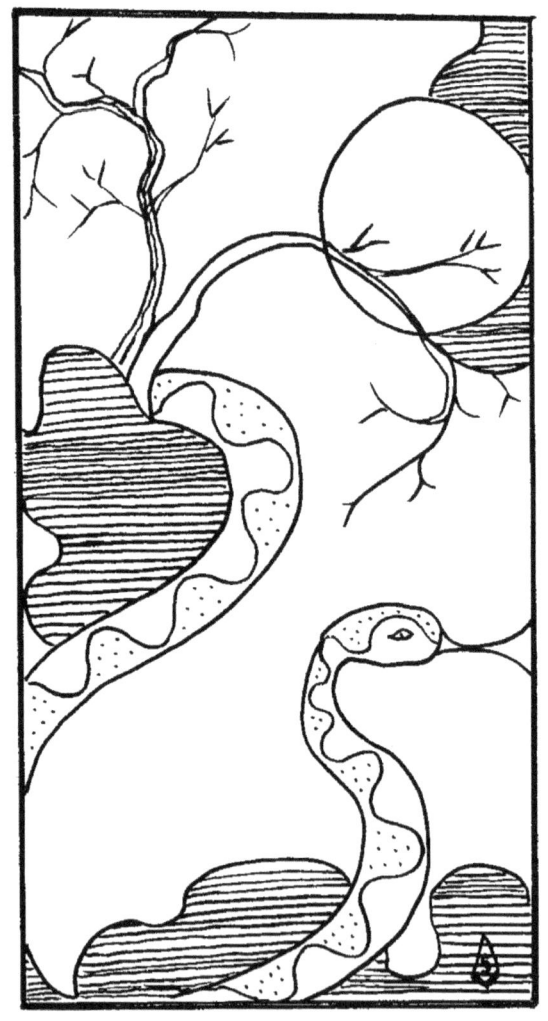

NATURE'S WAY

NATURE'S WAY

Nature's way is hard to understand.
All bamboos grow
Upright and strong.
Untended bamboos in woods
Grow upright and strong.
Needing no attention
Bamboos grow upright and strong.
Ah, children! children!

AFTER THE FREEZE

On the very first sunny day
After that too long a freeze
I took a heart-breaking survey
Of my beloved garden
Devastated beyond belief –
Limp grey foliage all around
Singed of its lively, uplifting green,
Mucky heaps of dead brown leaves,
Where bright heads of pretty blooms
Should predictably have been.

With a sigh I cried, "No more!
No more this yearly planting,
Waiting and tending, and finally witnessing
Such a ravaged scene. No more!"

And then ... and then...
Peeking between heaps of dead leaves
And inert, bruised branches
Lying pathetic on the ground
I saw the fresh unsullied green
Of Daffodil and Narcissus shoots,
Confident, hopeful, debonair.

Oh Lord! Lord, I see
Your swift and subtle ways here
To warm up with hopeful promise
My frost-bitten faith, as it were.

I picked up my rake and shovel,
Smoothed out my crumpled gloves
And pulled them briskly on.
And I picked up my spirit for happier days.

Lord, you truly are The Master Gardener,
With your mysterious ways.

APRIL

"April is the cruelest month of all
Mixing memory and desire"
Says T.S. Eliot, with whom I beg to differ.
For is not all of life a daily mix
Of memory and desire?

To me April is the most reassuring,
The most joyous month of all.
To see tender green leaves glistening
On seemingly dead branches
Is reason enough for delight and wonder.

Have you ever seen the saffron heart
Of a crocus, tulips bursting with color,
Dramatic amaryllis and pristine white lilies?
Have you heard sudden bird calls
Beckoning after a silent Winter?

If not, I urge you to take your leisure
In the garden, see the promise of life fulfilled,
And in your innermost being witness
A miracle unfolding and eager,
Faith in the future, year after year,

Though memories be sad, desires soured,
You will still find reason for gratitude,
For April with its flowers and showers,
Brings evidence of life renewed,
New vigorous life and life empowered.

THE WONDER OF GREEN

When Winter winds blow freezing cold
And when fog hangs a haze on the land
The fig tree even here in my southern garden
Stands leafless, a stark grey skeleton.

Patiently it stands through grey winter days,
Till at last, the sun moving to Summer Solstice,
Brings longer, warmer days,
Brings resurgence to those patient limbs
That now put out miracle green tips
At the end of those limbs, only seemingly sapless.

Then sooner than I thought, one day,
Returning from my morning walk,
I find the tree in green splendor,
Even bearing fruit known for sweetness
And therefore named Sweet Celeste,
Heavenly nectar.
When all seems hopeless and lost
In our lives too,
The sap still surges in you and me
As it does in that faith-filled, patient tree.

SPRING

Red rake
brown heaps of leaves
White Crocus crowns
in lilac light

WILD FLOWERS

While diligently tending my garden –
Planting and pruning,
Weeding, watering, fertilizing,
I wonder about those that ask for no devotion.
Yet bloom with joyful abandon,
Simply fulfilling their being,
Incidentally bringing delight
To passersby looking for them
Or weary travelers happily surprised.

Texas Blue Bonnet, Indian Paintbrush,
Wild Sunflower, Milkweed and many more
Radiant with joy under heaven,
Faithfully coming and going with the seasons
From birthing, blooming, dying, resurrecting.
Of wild flowers there is no dearth.
Does what goes for us humans
Apply to the lowly wild flowers too,
That the meek shall inherit the Earth?

Humbly indifferent to attention you go.
Wild flowers, I do love you so!

Sloughing in Autumn

           The snake, renewing
          in solitude,
         sloughs off dry
        worn-out skin
       still adhering,
      for one that's new,
     imperceptibly grown
    flawless under the old.
     In the light of the moon's
      full silver round, snake slows
       her liquid meandering way over
        dry leaves, coarse sun-burned stubble.
         The old skin grown familiar will not
          un-leech cleanly without rebellion,
           not without rubbing itself against
            rough-ridged rocks and bramble,
             gnarled knees of ancient trees.
              Rough paths alone help shed,
               grit and sharp bur spikes
                help cast off old clinger.
                 And she, free to glisten
                  now in her new self-sheen
                   under the waxing -waning,
                 age-old moon, is awesome
               In crisp listening stillness
              herself with herself.

NOVEMBER TREES IN THE POCONOS

Dark columns, bodies unadorned,
their lissome arms outstretched,
their red russet gold vestures
fallen billowing to their feet
with the north wind's impassioned
swooping whistling overtures.

Cathedral timbers arching high,
their charcoal-gray latticing
the unending white sheet of sky,
their parallel lines unparalleled,
stately portals to other worlds
where swift the winged mind may fly.

Awesome viewers of time present,
time past and time of leaves to come,
fluted sap touching trackless skies,
commissars of the constant earth,
Self-rooted, self-possessed,
indifferent to my ravished eyes.

MIST RISING

As I walk the trails at Crystal Lake
Nestled in the Poconos,
Grasmere and Windermere,
Snow-fringed Mansarovar,
Walden Pond, Tinker's Creek and many more
Are with me. And I ponder
If I'll ever be free of words that others wrote,
Like a child in nature, full of fresh wonder.

Then with the sun mounting higher,
The mist rises off the solid-seeming surface
of the lake, above the pink-crested hills,
Now the familiar landscape is seen anew
In the rising mist.
My eyes see it, my heart feels it.
Now a new tune plays in nature
Not anyone else's, but my own,
Tuned to my own soul stirrings.

In plain talk, though,
It was only the mist rising.

CLAUDE MONET AT GIVERNY

For thirty years you lived at Giverny
painting shimmering scenes of water gardens,
leaving behind all well-defined Impressionist art,
light and shade on scenes in perspective,
haystacks in the sun and sharp summer shadows,
ice on the Seine, fog on the Thames,
Camille in a green dress and scenes of Le Havre.

At Giverny, only water gardens with water lilies,
a stone bridge and willows trailing low
in homage to the scene, absorbed you,
as a single-passioned bee ravishes
a lone crocus in late winter.
Many a canvas now is this cool, watery spot,
a real and reflected encounter.

A contemplation too in dappled paint flow,
framed compositions in fluid strokes of blue,
green, pink, yellow and mystic indigo
reflect your soul's deep involvement,
and reach across vast distances of time
and space to hold me here entranced
by your timeless art, Monet at Giverny.

LESSONS FROM BIRDS

We call ourselves the crown of creation.
If we could but have humility,
A good measure of self-scrutiny,
We'd learn from other wonders of creation.

As we hike or bike in high places,
Or work in our cherished gardens,
We might learn from the many-splendored
Birds we chance to look upon.

Keen vision from hawks and eagles,
Vision when all is dark from owls,
Persistence from woodpeckers,
And focus from long-necked cranes.

Amazing faith from migrant birds,
Contentment from mourning doves.
Rhythms of rejoicing from peacocks,
And community spirit from pigeons.

Finches make any food a celebration.
Cardinals and robins herald happy days.
From swans we may learn serenity and grace,
From white doves, peaceful ways.

From many birds, true parenthood,
Day-long industry and vigilance.
We'd do well to rein in pride, and ponder,
Emulate in many ways the winged wonder.

TWO BIRDS

Two birds I watch at the river bank
Standing in the swirling shallows.
One twists and turns to either flank,
Preens her feathers, fusses and burrows.
The other, observant, sentry still,
Her face lifted up to the distant hill.

Two birds I have at once in me
Which more, which less I cannot say.
Yet this I hope most earnestly,
That deep within I focus more
Beyond my own every day chore,
On helping needy human beings,
And find in that selfless endeavor
Peace and bliss for ever more.

THE CAMEO DRAMA

I see as the sun rises
a drama of moments transpire.
Birds swoop down from barren trees
that stand tall in the pink sky.
They flit and hop in the grass,
they peck for insects and seeds,
they trill like a practiced choir.
It seems they own the woods and sky.
Then suddenly the pink light dims,
grey clouds the prospect overcast,
raindrops fall fast upon the grass.
The birds all quickly disappear
and leave me alone to wonder
whether all that brisk, brief drama
of darting here, there, everywhere
for food and play and proud broadcast,
so shrill with small discoveries
of comedies and tragedies
was a cameo of human endeavors.

ZEBRAS

Zebras hypnotize me.
They are too soft-contoured to be
sinewy as horses at a gallop,
Too squarely compact to be
elegant as giraffes on the horizon,
Too dramatic in stripes to elude or awe
like lions in a tawny landscape,
Too gregarious and earth-bound to soar
like eagles singly in the sky.

No zebra ever said, "I wish I were."
They accept themselves.
Zebras do not compete.
They run free, all together,
Thirty kilometers an hour
and graze satisfied.

ZAZEN

Pond water glistens
reflecting the vast blue sky.
Goldfish glide red gold
under resplendent lily pads,
then stand still in water
seemingly effortless.
Street sounds stop
at lily pond's edge.
I on my garden seat
no longer want to zoom around,
for I find the whole world
and the boundless beyond
in my own backyard.

THE DEW'S FAREWELL

The sun calls at my door
and I am ready to depart.
Green grass and lovely flower
that I fondly clung to,
luscious leaf, sweet-scented air,
farewell to you.
And pardon me that
with an unflinching heart
so happily I tower
from you whom I loved before.
A former impassioned lover
becomes a detached observer -
morning dew
arises as vapor.
I know mine is not mine
I know i am not I.
If only, like the dew,
I could arise and go
Into cosmic ecstasy.
Sans boundary.

GRASS LINKS

Grass grows with invincible life
From under paved paths,
In proper lawns, in wide open fields,
Wherever grass seeds fall.

Amaryllis and Tulips bloom
In carefully tended flower beds
For three short weeks in Spring
To the admiration of all.

Amaryllis and Tulips shrink
Into their separate bulbs
Through most of the year,
Self-absorbed, indifferent to all.

Gregarious grass, though,
In rough or fine weather,
Through drought or rain,
Keeps reaching out to all.

With quiet, invincible life,
This lowly connector
Links one blade with another,
And the other with all.

TREES – MY TEACHERS

To grow, to be
Ever reaching upward as the palm.
Come beating rain, come lashing wind
Or mighty swirling hurricane
Tearing green fronds.
To bear it all, still standing tall.
Then upright in the face of the sun,
Finally, and unfailingly appearing,
To shake out wounded fronds
To look hopefully at the golden globe
Of promise after heavy rain
To stand upright, forgetful of pain,
To stand thus, smiling.

To grow, to be
Maturing into fullness as the mango tree,
Fragrant with white blossoms in the Spring,
Laden with ripening fruit in the Summer,
Offering sweetness with firmness,
Nourishment for one and all.
Thus, to be a beneficent giver
Laden with goodness while bending low,
Regal in humility.

To grow, to be
All-embracing as the ancient banyan tree
Poised in uninterrupted movement
From root to branch and branch to root
On aerial resurrectors asserting life.
Old and gnarled, young and smooth,
All striving for new reaches
As one continuous being,
Intuiting growth toward eternal life.

To grow so, to be.
That is all.

CONTEMPLATIONS

AWAKENING

I swing in the cocoon of my own making
As most others do, in a world contrite.
Self-centered, self-absorbed,
And, therefore, always self-serving.

I hope some day the somnambulant being
Wakes, intuiting the light all around,
Breaks out of enclosed ignorance
Into uplifting, purposeful recognition.
No longer self-centered.
No longer self-absorbed.
No longer cocoon-bound.
Then spreading stirred up humane wings
Takes flight, spreading love and joy all around.

CAMERA EYE

The scope of my lens limits me.
I am sensitive to light and shade
There must be just so much of each
for me to be me.
I gather the prospect through my lens –
The image stands on its head
Inverted by my pinhole aperture
demanding right light
right distance and full poise –
all for a finite frame.
Happenstance,
someday this image snatcher
the eye of my soul
may open wide, wider
and see no inversions
but simply what is as it is.

HEAVEN

Exquisite light
if heaven is like this
I have seen it
dark awesome cloud
if heaven is like this
this I have found
opposites
and everything in between
that must be it.

IN THE FACE OF THE STARS

4,500 stars are visible to the naked eye,
2,000,000 through a telescope.
The Milky Way is only a miniscule part of
Twenty galaxies of Milky Ways
In a radius of 1,500,000 light years.
Electronic telescopes show more, much more –
30 billion stars in our Milky Way alone.
And Life?
Possibly 18,000 inhabited planets.
2,000,000 species of living things.
And I?
Upon our planet this Earth – an ordinary
Star of unimpressive size
In vast unthinkable cosmic space
I, undistinguished on this continent
Or state or city, township or street.
Yet, If I can be the best
that I can be,
a human being can be,
It matters not at all
How vast the greatest galaxy.

LETTING GO

So much is written in shifting sand
Upon the long beach of the mind
So much is written of involvement
Over and over, meaning is hard to find.

The ocean's incoming rhythmic tides
Wash out the inscrutably scribbled strand
Making immaculate, simple, receptive
The once furrowed brow of the ample sand.

So in meditation the tide of breath
Exhales I-ness, toxins of attachment,
Inhales energy, peace of here and now
On the clean-swept mind-shore of detachment.

Ocean says be intimate with the world-shore,
But let go more and more, and more and more.

THE MEASURING ROD

From embryo
    to ashes
        is an ambiguous measure.
It is nothing to nothing
    or almost so.
Or something to something
    or not quite so.
The question is
    how much is
        almost to almost
In ten thousand
    games of touch-n-go
Whether from growth to growth
    or status quo?

SPEAKING OF ANCHORS

Big boats and little boats
And boats that turn
With the tide and twirl.
But of all the boats there are,
This is a strange one sure
That on the placid water
Must bob and turn and twirl.

There is a wheel
That I try to steer.
There is a compass too.
But even in calm weather
It does unreasonably reel.

The wise say
There is an anchor
That can be lowered down
Through the flowing water
Onto the steadfast ground.

But of little use
Is the anchor
To the one who is lost at sea,
And of little use
Is the anchor
If the rope of centered steadfastness
Falls short, much too short.

THE SENSES AND THE SELF

So I touch the smooth gravel of your voice
Hear the whispered anecdotes of your eyes
See the vibrant palette of your heart
Smell the lingering musk of your smile
Taste the hot and subtle spices of your touch
Rest in the restlessness of self searching for self

WALKING OUT

Rain pelting down on hot June nights
Raises spirit moving smells of earth
There is an urge to rise and seek
Some place where senses cease,
Where ships tossed in Monsoon storms
May find a cove and rest in peace.
For rain-washed air and fragrant earth
Raise curtains on
Transitoriness.
When earth and sky consummate
And the sense of being accentuate,
There is a call from beyond mind's guess
And the wakeful soul's unrest.
Something is born
That instantly rises
Peers out the door
And goes into the night
To walk on water
Alone. Free. Embracing all.

WHERE NO WIND BLOWS

Hush! wild roving mind
bringer of past pain,
conjurer of days to be,
the all computing bane.
Seek shelter
in the windless place
where now alone is clear,
the place where
last night weeps no more
and tomorrow is no sore.

Hush! wild rover,
bringer of all trivia,
conjurer of otherness,
I and my myopia.
Seek shelter
in the windless place
where love grows sheer,
the place where
I weeps not for I
And "mine" will disappear.

Hush! wild rover,
bringer of divisions,
conjurer with pros and cons
and corporeal concessions.
Seek shelter
in the windless place
where the flame shines clear,
the place where
flickers no self-shadow,
only the Self's Self-glow.

THE CHALLENGE

Early in life, or later
There comes a challenge.
Like scaling a mountain peak
Often without adequate gear.
Just everyday shoes, gripless gloves,
No hook or hauling rope,
No safety net to stop a fall.
In every step, no security at all.

But if faith be the studs on boots,
And hope the strong hauling rope,
He who makes the dumb to speak
And the lame to climb the mountain peak,
Will make the challenge surmountable
And life, as always, cherishable.

THE FALL GARDENER

It is not winter yet
But summer's gone
And I keep looking for
Sweet, mellowing autumn fruit,
Dream oranges weighing down the boughs.
So many promises everywhere
But not one full-grown fruit.

The tender of trees
With shaking head explains,
"Nature's way is profusion,
 Sending out branch after branch.
Without lopping, pruning, guarding
Little of worth can come.
Good fruit needs cultivation."

It is not winter yet
But summer's gone
And for all the lopping,
Pruning, guarding I would do,
Of what loss there's been
Through idle shears,
I still must do the reckoning.

Yet, the only ultimate reckoning
Must be the invisible pruning
And subtle shaping of the spirit.
It must be vigilant action,
So that what I cultivate
In my soul's ample garden
At last finds sweet fruition.

PERSPECTIVE

Of cosmic time, this my life
Not even a half wink of Brahma's eye.
For a 1,000,000 x 1,000,000 years
Is still a fraction of His one awesome wink.
Scholars declare themselves, myself,
All of us – homo sapiens –
At the crest of creation,
Paragons of progress,
Our age, the acme of achievement.
They trace events in time
"From the very beginning."
Cultural historians claim
They debate more than dates and places
And lessons of history. They say:
"We go deep, deeper than scholars before us.
We cross cultural boundaries.
We are interdisciplinary.
Myopic no more, we scan global issues;
We are aware of the larger space,
The greater time span."

As for me,
I scan not infinity with finite thought,
Probe not eternity from numbered days.
I sit silent,
Emptying thought.

THE SONG OF THE STONE

Breaking loose, alone, I ask
What and where and how and why.
Seeking the great Reality,
Infinitesimal i am I.

As now I've tumbled at your feet
Pure Waters, wash away the grime.
Let me find in you my rest
With a final adieu to rolling time.

So flood me wisdom's waters
That nothing of this stone remains,
When, as water in the waters
The promised state of bliss attains.

TOWARD SILENCE

From ocean-mind's unfathomed depths where waves
Rise into daily skies of consciousness
And press in sustained clamor to the shore
There to crash and come again more and more

From ocean-mind's ceaseless roar I hope
One day I turn into a pool as tremorless
As mighty Jhelum's Himalayan Source
Where fish may swim in waters still as glass.

I hope showers of the world's hard pebbles
Dropped into my lake's clear consciousness
Make not a sound. Only pebble-rings in silence
Skim the surface of my lake's effulgence

And disappear. Below will be silence.
Before, during, after – wakeful silence.

GOURDS AND HUMANS

Gourds and squashes have a way
Of starting imperceptibly
At the base of flowers on the vine,
As humans do in their mother's womb.

Gourds grow in fullness under the sun
Only in a few week's time.
Human life is more variable,
Unpredictable from womb to tomb.

Some gourds and squashes provide food,
Some decorative delight in the Fall,
Some get carved into birdhouses and bowls.
There is fulfillment of being for all.

And gourds left uncut on the vine, mature
With a legacy of seeds, and then ease
Pain free, soundlessly off the vine
And lie upon the earth in peaceful release.

Would that all human life
Could find such useful service,
Give unselfish delight and at the final hour
Come off the vine of life pain free, in peace.

THE LOTUS

The lotus seed lies in the muck
At the bottom of the placid pond.
Down there, somehow in the dark,
With the weight of the water upon its chest,
It knows beyond a doubt that up there
Exists a thing called light, the spark
That kindles life, the source of all
Here, hereafter and evermore.
It has that same pristine knowledge,
Beyond the this and that of knowledge,
That unshakeable thing called faith.

Oh lotus! Lotus, with your amazing faith,
Come dwell and bloom in my heart.
Take me ever upward to the abode of grace,
Untainted, untroubled by the waters of life,
Ever resplendent in the here and now.
Come lotus! Come! Bloom in my heart.

MEDITATION

I hope one day
Pebbles dropped into my lake's deep waters
Will make not a sound.
Ring after ring
Skimming the surface
Will ripple to the shore of my consciousness
And disappear.
Below,
In the depths,
In the fullness of being ...
Silence
Before, during, after ...
Silence.

Sita Kapadia, Ph.D., is Professor Emeritus of English and World Literature, City University of New York. Sita's teaching career in the USA began in 1971. Before that, she had been a professor in India and Malaysia. At her college in New York, in addition to the standard classes in English Language, Literature, and Creative Writing, she pioneered classes in English as a Second Language (ESL), Early Asian Literature and Modern Asian Literature.

She has presented several literary papers at universities in India and the USA, including at an international conference at Harvard University. Her critical articles have been published in McGill's Encyclopedia of Literary Criticism and her poems in anthologies. Sita's book, *The Woman Beside Gandhi, A Biography of Kasturba, Wife of the Mahatma*, was published in 2020.

Multi-talented, Sita is a writer, poet, artist and master gardener. In "retirement", she has taught Hinduism and Creative Writing. At the Jaipur Literature Festival, Houston, she was a presenter at two events. She is also an occasional speaker at the Eternal Gandhi Museum Houston.

www.ingramcontent.com/pod-product-compliance
Lightning Source LLC
Chambersburg PA
CBHW061739070526
44585CB00024B/2733